KENYA
is my country

Bernice and Cliff Moon

Wayland

My Country

America is my country
Australia is my country
Britain is my country
China is my country
Denmark is my country
France is my country
Greece is my country
India is my country
Israel is my country
Italy is my country
Kenya is my country
New Zealand is my country
Spain is my country

Further titles are in preparation

This book is based on We live in Kenya *by Zulf M. Khalfan and Mohamed Amin.*

First published in 1985 by
Wayland (Publishers) Ltd
49 Lansdowne Place, Hove
East Sussex BN3 1HF, England

ISBN 0 85078 489 1

Filmset by Latimer Trend & Company Ltd, Plymouth
Printed in Italy by G. Canale & C.S.p.A., Turin
Bound in the UK by The Pitman Press, Bath

Contents

I am Phoebe and I'm a Member of Parliament.

Kenya is in East Africa and our parliament
is called the National Assembly.
There are 158 MPs in the National Assembly.
I am the MP for Karachuonyo which is on
the eastern shores of Lake Victoria.
I enjoy meeting people and helping them with their problems.
People are always asking me to give them jobs, food,
better health care or somewhere to live.
We try to get them to help themselves if they are able to.
For example, out of every 1,000 babies born in Karachuonyo,
about a quarter die of malaria or other illnesses.
So the government is trying to show people how important it is
to wash themselves carefully and to keep their houses clean.

Kenya is my country

In this book 26 people from all over Kenya tell you what their life is like—life in the cities, life in the bushlands and life on the farms.

SUDAN
ETHIOPIA
UGANDA
SOMALIA
TANZANIA
INDIAN OCEAN
Lake Turkana
(L. Rudolf)
Moyale
Eastern Province
Marsabit
North-Eastern Province
Mt. Elgon
Kitale
Western Province
Nandi Forest
Lake Baringo
Aberdare Mountains
Meru
Mt. Kenya
Kakamega
Eldoret
Kapsabet
Central Province
Kisumu
Nakuru
Lake Victoria
Kericho
Nyanza Province
Kisii
Limuru
Kiambu
Sotik
Nairobi
Machakos
Rift Valley Province
River Athi
Coast Province
River Tana
Lamu
Mt. Kilimanjaro
Taita Hills
Tsavo
River Galana
Malindi
Kilifi
Mombasa

This is our parliament.
It is in Nairobi which is
the capital of Kenya.
At the moment there are
only four women MPs but
I am trying to make women
more important in Kenya.

We have a general election
every five years in Kenya.
These two Masai people
are putting their votes
into the metal ballot box.

My name is Martin and I am a train driver.

When I first started working for the Kenyan Railways Corporation I drove a steam engine and it was a very hot job. Now I drive a diesel train and it's much more comfortable.

Kenyan Railways have about 330 trains and in 1981 we carried more than 2,000,000 passengers. This railway was built about 90 years ago.

We still use steam engines for some goods trains.
This train is travelling through a very lonely part of Kenya.

One of the most exciting journeys in Kenya
is the train ride from Mombasa to Uganda.
You start by the sea at Mombasa and then you ride
through the Tsavo National Park and the Athi Plains.
You can see every kind of Kenyan wildlife from the windows.
Then the railway climbs 900 metres (3,000 feet) to Limuru.
It drops down into the Great Rift Valley
and then climbs again.
Eventually the train reaches the banana plantations of Uganda.

I am Athman.
I'm a curator.

A curator is a person who is in charge of a museum
and I'm the curator of the Lamu Museum.
Lamu is a group of islands near the coast of Kenya.

I work in other places too.
I am in charge of
this excavation at Siyo Fort
on Siyu Island, off Lamu.
Today we are digging up
old cannons near the fort.

We have two rainy seasons in Kenya.
The 'long' rains come between March and May when it rains very heavily for about $2\frac{1}{2}$ months.
The 'short' rains come between October and November when it rains for about 6 weeks.
I work in the museum when it rains but during the rest of the year I work outdoors.
I cover a wide area along the coast from the border with Somalia to the delta of the River Tana.

I have to look after many old buildings like this 400-year-old Portuguese fort on Lamu.

I am Kibiy and I'm an elder of my tribe.

There are about forty tribes in Kenya.
I am an elder of the Nandi Tribe.
Young people in my tribe come to me to talk about our way of life and sometimes they ask me for advice.

I live near the Nandi Forest in the Rift Valley Province in this little mud-and-grass thatched house.

The soil around here is very rich and so we are farmers.
We grow millet, maize, beans, potatoes, tobacco, bananas, sorghum and pyrethrum.
Sorghum is a grass and we use it to make hay for our cattle.
Pyrethrum is a chrysanthemum and we dry the flowers to make chemicals for killing insects.
We also keep sheep and cattle on our small farms.

Here I am with one of my cows.
She is very healthy and I am proud of her.
I have twenty cattle altogether on my farm.
Cattle are as important to us as money is to you.

I am Mwangi and I sell medicines.

I live in Nairobi where I sell medicines made from herbs. Every day I set out my medicine stall under a shady tree. In Kenya there are many people like me who make and sell herbal medicines.

My stall is under a tree near Nairobi bus station.
Lots of people come here each day.
They stand in the shade under my tree to wait for their buses.

My father taught me how to make medicines from plants.
People come to me if they have a headache or backache and sometimes they take my medicines if they have an upset tummy.
I use many kinds of plants as well as the branches, roots and bark of trees.
Sometimes I make powders which must be taken with tea or soup.
Once I had a very bad cough so I tried a medicine which my grandfather used to make.
I sent my friend to get the branch and root I needed.
I boiled them up and drank three spoonfuls of the juice.
Then I had a long sleep and I've never had the cough since.

My name is David. I grow coffee.

How often do you have a cup of coffee?
Coffee is made from beans which grow on a coffee plant.
I have 90,000 coffee plants on my farm at Kiambu which is 1,800 metres (5,700 feet) above sea level in the Central Province of Kenya.

After we have picked all the beans we put them on long tables to dry in the sun.

We pick the coffee beans
twice a year.
The first crop is picked
in May or June and
the second crop is picked
in November or December.
We need lots of workers
to help pick the beans
and mothers often bring
their children with them.

Kiambu is right in the middle of Kenya's coffee-growing area.
Every year we send about 100 tonnes of coffee beans
to the people who sell them for us.
There is plenty of rich farmland in Kenya but
nowadays most of the farms are small.
Next time you go shopping, look out for packets of coffee beans.
You might see some packets of Kenyan coffee beans.

I'm Eunice and I'm an editor.

My magazine is called the *Consumer's Digest*.
Kenyans can buy many kinds of magazines and newspapers.
They may be written in English, German or Swahili.
In Kenya a lot of people speak Swahili.
Every day there are five different newspapers on sale.
Three of them are printed in English and two in Swahili.

This is my family.
We are sitting in
our garden in Nairobi.

Most Kenyan farm-workers are women.
My magazine tries to show what women are doing
to make Kenya a better country.

Away from the towns many people cannot read or write.
They keep in touch with the news by listening to the radio.
It is called the Voice of Kenya or VOK for short.
Programmes can be in English, Swahili or in one of the many
other languages which are spoken in Kenya.

I am George.
I'm a minister.

At Christmas we have
a tall decorated tree
in a park in Nairobi.
Children love to come
and see it.
It is sunny and warm
in Kenya at Christmas so
our Christmas isn't the same
as in northern countries.

I am the minister of St. Andrew's Church in Nairobi.
There are many different religions in Kenya.
In Nairobi we have Hindu and Sikh temples as well as Christian churches and Muslim mosques.
Christian missionaries first came to Kenya in 1844.
They taught people how to read and write, how to farm and how to look after their health.
They also taught people to be carpenters or masons.
Many Indians came to Kenya after the Christian missionaries and they helped to build the Kenya–Uganda Railway.
The Indians brought their own religions to our country.

Pope John Paul II came to visit Kenya.
Here he is, preaching in Nairobi Cathedral.

I am Elphas and I'm a schoolboy.

I'm in the third year at a secondary school in Nairobi.
My home is a farm in Kakamega, Western Province.
That is a long way from Nairobi.
My mother and my brothers and sisters live there but
I live with my father in a flat in Nairobi.

These women are buying bananas in the main street of Kakamega.
I go back to Kakamega during the holidays in April, August and December.

This is the primary school
I went to in Kakamega
before I came to Nairobi.
We used to stand
in a circle around
the Kenyan flag for
our morning assembly.

I shall take my exams in one year's time.
If I pass them I can go into the sixth form.
I spent seven years at primary school but
not all Kenyan children go to school.
The government is spending a great deal on education and
is trying to make sure that every child goes to school.

Kakamega has a lot of rain during the first half of the year
and during the second half it doesn't rain at all.
This kind of climate is very good for growing maize,
cotton, coffee, sugar-cane and tea.

I am Kennedy and I carve soapstone.

My father was a soapstone carver and I used to play
with the chips from his carvings when I was four years old.
I began carving small things like fishes and eggs as I grew older.
My father used to help me and soon I learnt to carve
bigger things like cups and birds.
I live in a village near Kisii in Nyanza Province.
I get my soapstone from a quarry about 10 km (6 miles) away.
I have to carry the stone on my head all the way
from the quarry to my home.
I use a large knife called a *panga* to cut the stone
into the rough shape of the thing I want to carve.
Then I carve the stone with a small knife called a *kisu*.
When the carving is finished I wash it, polish it with sandpaper
and then clean it with a brush.

This is my family.
We are in front
of the hut where
the children sleep.

These men are sawing up soapstone at the quarry
in the hills near my home.
You can get white, black and pink soapstone but
most people like pink soapstone the best.

I am Jackson. I'm a tea-picker.

Millions of people enjoy drinking tea.
Tea from Kenya is well known all over the world.
You get tea from the leaves of a small bush.
The leaves are dried and cut up into tiny pieces.

Tea-pickers have to weigh their baskets of leaves. The more tea they pick, the more money they earn.

Here is a large field of tea bushes.
The bushes grow in neat lines and their leaves are shiny.
The pickers work in rows from one end of the field to the other.
They pick only the top two leaves of each tea plant's shoots.

I pick tea on a tea farm near Kapsabet in Nandi District.
Kericho, Sotik and Nandi are the oldest tea-growing areas.
In Kericho there is an old Tea Hotel which must serve
the freshest tea in the world.

My name is Sam. I'm a park warden.

I am a warden at Nairobi National Park which is a wildlife park only a short distance from Nairobi's busy city centre.

Here you can see me playing with Kambe, a baby cheetah who has hurt a front paw. We will look after Kambe until the paw is better.

We have about 40 wildlife parks in Kenya.
Nairobi National Park covers 113 square kilometres (44 square miles).
The animals in our park were not brought here.
They have always lived in this part of Kenya and they can wander wherever they like just as they always have done.
There are lions, cheetahs, rhinos, buffaloes, ostriches and zebras.
I am the warden in charge of the animal orphanage where we look after injured or sick animals as well as abandoned baby animals.
At the moment we have about 300 animals in the orphanage.
We are open to visitors but we are not a zoo—the animals are here only because they need our help and protection.

Nairobi National Park is very close to the city.

I am Mildred and I'm a bank manager.

I am a manager with the National Bank of Kenya.
Our bank is owned by the Kenyan government.
There are many other banks in Kenya—some are European, some Asian, some American and some Arab-owned.

This is my family outside our Nairobi home. I was born near Kisumu in Nyanza Province but I was a student at Nairobi University. I got a job at the bank as soon as I passed my degree in commerce.

This is the head office of the National Bank of Kenya in Nairobi. This is where I work. The bank was set up in 1968. It has four branches in Nairobi and there are also branches in Mombasa, Eldoret, Nakuru and Kisumu. I was the first woman manager to be taken on by the bank but now there are many more women in banking.

Large businesses tend to use foreign and private banks but the National Bank of Kenya is used by ordinary Kenyans. We are owned by the people and we work for the people.

I am Ahmed. I'm a poet.

This man is making
a model of a boat
called a *dhow*.
He lives on the island
of Lamu off the coast
of Kenya.
I was born on Lamu
but now I live and work
as a clerk in Mombasa.
I still visit Lamu and
I often see this man
selling his models to tourists.

This man is building a full-sized *dhow*.
A *dhow* is a kind of sailing boat and I once wrote a poem about how they are made.

My grandmother was a well-known Swahili poet.
I can still remember her singing and reading her poems.
I write poems in the Swahili language too.
My grandmother trained me and when I was only 12
I started to write my own poems.
When she had too much work she let me help
by writing poems for her.
People who live on Lamu like to hear a poem
whenever there is a wedding, a funeral or a birth.
I am the poet who writes the poems for them.

I am Jayantilal and I am a businessman.

I used to live in India until I came to Kenya in 1950.
I work in the family firm my uncle started 60 years ago.
My family likes living in Kenya and we don't miss India.
Our children were brought up in Kenya.
Now they are married and they feel they belong to this country.

Here I am at home with my wife and two daughters. We live in a five-bedroomed bungalow on the outskirts of Nairobi.

My firm sells furniture, fabrics and carpets.
I try to choose attractive colours and patterns and everything is made to a very high standard.
I work long hours and I have to be careful about how I spend the money I earn.
My family has been in this trade for a long time now and we know which goods will sell best.
My customers know that they can trust me and that what they buy will be of good quality.

This is Biashara Street in Nairobi where we have our shop.
Biashara is the Swahili word for 'business'.

My name is Eric.
I'm a doctor.

The Kenyan health service has become much better in recent years.
In 1981 there were 221 hospitals, 262 health centres
and 1,100 chemists.
The number of doctors and dentists has risen too.
Most Kenyan doctors have private practices
where you have to pay for treatment, but many of them also do
some work for the government health service.
I have a private practice in Nairobi but I also work
once a week at the Kenyatta National Hospital.
People in Kenya can get free treatment when they are ill and
most people live near a hospital.
But there are long waiting lists for free treatment so
people come to a private practice like mine if they can afford it.
The illnesses we treat are usually malaria, diarrhoea,
sleeping sickness, stomach illnesses and hook worm.

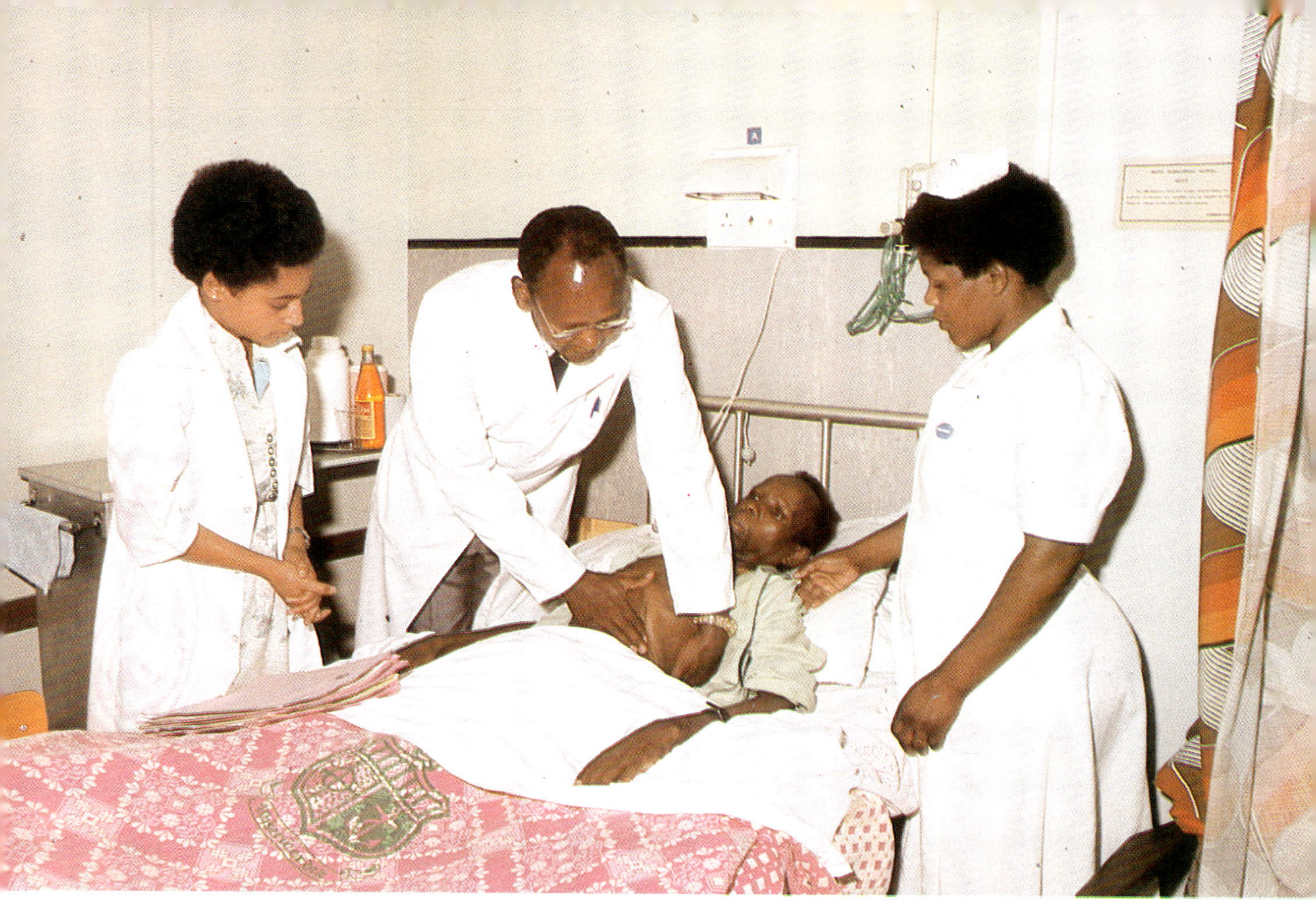

This is my clinic at the Kenyatta National Hospital in Nairobi. Here I am examining one of my patients.

These are the Taita Hills where I have a small farm. I like to come here to relax at weekends.

I am Timothy and I sell souvenirs.

I sell souvenirs from a street stall in Nairobi. Tourists who visit Nairobi like to take a souvenir back with them to remind them of their visit to Kenya. I sell baskets, masks and carvings of elephants, rhinos and leopards.

People who buy my souvenirs find that they are cheaper than those in the shops.

Here is a famous wood-carver working in front of his home.
His wife and son are watching him work.

Most of the wood carvings I sell are made
by the Wakamba tribe who live in the Eastern Province.
They live in a part of Kenya which often suffers from drought
so they make carvings to earn themselves money to buy food.
Many tourists think that my carvings are made by machines
because they are so well finished, but they're all made by hand.
I like to tell them why a particular souvenir was carved and
I also remind them to put oil on the carving
so that the wood will not be damaged by the hot sun.

I am Ramadhan.
I am an imam.

An *imam* is a person who leads the worship in a mosque where Muslims go to say their prayers.
Muslims pray five times a day—at dawn, in the afternoon, in the evening, at dusk and at night.
I am the *imam* of the Jamia Mosque which is a very beautiful building in the centre of Nairobi.
About 6 per cent of the people in Kenya are Muslims.
Muslims believe that there is one God, called Allah, and that Mohammed is his prophet.
Our Holy Book is called the Koran and I was only 7 years old when I started to read it.
I have studied Islam, the Muslim religion, all my life.

This is the Jamia Mosque in Nairobi.
Muslims come here once a week for the Friday prayers.
Tourists also visit the mosque and many come to talk to me.

This was once a city called Shanga.
It was built by the first Muslims who came to Kenya.

My name is Lucy. I'm a student.

I am 24 years old and I'm a student at Nairobi University. I am studying for a degree in commerce and I hope to work for a market research firm when I have passed my exams.

This is Nairobi University. It is the only university in Kenya and it is very modern.

In 1956 Nairobi University started as a technical college
for teaching engineering and business studies.
In 1970 it became the only university in Kenya.
There are about 7,000 students altogether.
In the past girls were not given any education.
They were expected to stay at home
until they got married.
Now things are changing and
about one-third of the students here are girls.

This is graduation day at Nairobi University.

My name is Alex. I'm a fisherman.

I live near Kisumu which is on the shore
of Lake Victoria in Nyanza Province.
Lake Victoria is huge—the largest lake in Africa and
the second largest in the world.
I catch most of my fish with long fishing lines.
I use a line with about 400 hooks on it to catch Nile perch.
There are plenty of Nile perch in Lake Victoria and
they are delicious to eat.
They can weigh up to 100 kilos (220 lbs).
Some of the sardine fishermen around here use gill nets
which look like mosquito nets but are expensive to buy.
Other fishermen use seine nets which are much bigger.
They take five or six seine nets out in a boat
and drop them in a circle.
Then two gangs of men pull them in to the shore,
trapping the fish that get caught in the nets.

Here are some of my friends who fish in Lake Victoria.
Most of Kenya's freshwater fish are caught here.

It is the end of a day's fishing. The fishermen are laying out their nets by the side of the lake.

I am Charles and I am a safari guide.

These tourists are going
on safari by balloon.
It is the best way
to see Kenya's wildlife.
They will see lions,
antelopes, elephants
and rhinos.
I can't take people
on balloon safaris but
I can drive them around
Kenya's national parks.

This is Mount Kenya which is 5,117 metres (17,058 feet) high.
It is in the Aberdare Mountains and
almost every tourist comes to see it.

I often take tourists to the Aberdare National Park.
There are two famous lodges in the park called Treetops
and The Ark where you can watch wildlife during the day
and by floodlight at night.
I sometimes take people to Amboseli National Park
where they can see Mount Kilimanjaro.
Most of the park is flat so I can drive off the road
and get very close to the animals.

I am Abdullah. I'm a herdsman.

I live near Moyale in the Eastern Province.
I keep about 20 cattle and 50 goats.
I keep them in a *boma* which is a piece of land with a fence all round it.
The fence is made of dried thorn bushes.
It can get very hot up here especially in January when the temperature can be 30°C (86°F).
I get up before 6 a.m. while it's still cool and check the *boma* to make sure that all my animals are safe.
Sometimes lions or cheetahs attack them.
If I hear an attack I run out with a spear to scare the wild animal away.
But it's hard to scare an animal if it has already killed its next meal.
Wild animals don't give up a meal that easily.

In our part of Kenya
people use camels
to carry things
from village to village.

We often have to drive our cattle to places
where there is food for them to eat.

My name is Omar and I own a restaurant.

My restaurant is called Malindi Dishes and you'll find it on the outskirts of Nairobi. I am well known for my Swahili dishes. The food is usually cooked in a rich sauce made from coconut milk.

I have to make sure that my cook doesn't burn the kebabs on the barbecue.

Do you like your food salty or sweet?
You can buy both in my restaurant.
I have dishes made from bananas, beans, peas and cassava.
I also make snacks from rice, wheat and bean flours.
You can buy a rice cake or a sweet pastry.
I make curry, fish dishes, kebabs and barbecued chicken.
I also serve wild spinach as a vegetable.
For pudding you can have pumpkin, sweet potatoes,
strips of green pawpaw cooked in milk, and
balls of wheat dough, deep-fried in oil and covered with syrup.

I often help to serve the food in my restaurant.

I am Joseph and I'm an art collector.

I used to be the Vice-President of Kenya but now
I'm 71 and I've retired from politics.
My shop in Nairobi sells pictures and sculptures by African artists.

Politicians drive out to the villages at election time
and everyone gathers to hear their speeches.

I have works of art
from the whole of Africa
in my art collection.
I also collect art
from Europe and China.
Just look at this
fine African wood carving.
We must do more
to help African artists
to carry on making
such beautiful things.
And we must make sure
that African works of art
don't all get sold
to other countries.
The Kenyan government
has bought my collection
so now it will be kept
in this country.

My collection keeps me very busy most of the time but I also enjoy relaxing at my ranch in Nyanza Province.

I am Joseph and I'm a matatu driver.

Matatu is the Swahili name for a minibus.
My *matatu* can carry 22 people.
It's 12 years old so I have to look after it.
Most of the time I take people to and from work in Nairobi.
I always try to get my passengers to work on time because
I don't like people getting angry when they're late for work.
Matatus can often take short cuts which larger buses can't manage
and once they're full, *matatus* don't stop.
On a good day I can carry up to 700 passengers—
that's if the minibus doesn't break down!

At the end of the day
I pick up my passengers
to take them home from work.

I hope this *matatu*
has a strong roof rack.

I am Amina.
I'm a student.

I am 18 years old and I study at the Kenya Polytechnic in Nairobi.
This is my second year and I am training to be a secretary.
We can train to be secretaries in law or health
or as a private secretary or an audio-typist.
I am on a course for secretaries who will work in the health service.
Other students take courses in engineering, science, printing,
management and commerce.
I really like the polytechnic and the other students here.
It helps to have people from different tribes and
different parts of the country in one place because
we learn to understand each other better.

This is the Kenya Polytechnic in Nairobi.
The only other polytechnic is in Mombasa.

It is lunchtime and we are getting ready
for our afternoon classes.

Facts

Capital city	The capital city of Kenya is Nairobi.
Language	Most people in Kenya speak Swahili but 75 other languages are also spoken.
Money	Kenyans pay for things with cents, shillings and pounds. There are 100 cents in one Kenya shilling and 20 Kenya shillings in one Kenya pound.
Religion	Kenyans can go to any church they like. A quarter of the people are Christians. There are also Muslims and Hindus.
People	Kenya has many small towns with about 3,000 to 10,000 people living in each of them. Very few people live in the northern half of the country. Most Kenyans are African but there are also Asians, Europeans and Arabs in Kenya. There are also more than 40 different tribes.
Weather	Where the land is above 1,500 metres (5,000 ft) the weather is rainy and mild. The north of the country is very dry. The coast is hot and damp.

Government On 12 December 1964, Kenya became a republic.
Its parliament is called the National Assembly and it has 172 members.
Kenya has a President and is a one-party state.

Houses Housing is a big problem in Kenya.
Houses in the countryside are usually very poor.
In the towns there are not enough houses.

Schools Children do not have to go to school.
The government is trying to help adults who cannot read or write.

Farming Coffee, tea, sisal, pyrethrum, maize and wheat are grown in the highlands.
Coconuts, cashew nuts, cotton, sugar, sisal and maize are grown in the lowlands.

Factories Kenya's factories make beer, soft drinks, flour, medicines, clothing, cigarettes, canned fruit and meat and coffee products.

News Kenyan radio is called the Voice of Kenya (VOK).
A television service was started in 1962.
There are 5 daily and 5 weekly newspapers.

Index